EDITOR: MARTIN WINDROW

 MEN-AT-ARMS SERIES 113

THE ARMIES OF AGINCOURT

Text and colour plates by
CHRISTOPHER ROTHERO

First published in Great Britain in 1981 by
Osprey, an imprint of Reed Consumer Books Ltd.
Michelin House, 81 Fulham Road,
London SW3 6RB
and Auckland, Melbourne, Singapore and Toronto

ISBN 0 85045 394 1

Filmset in Great Britain
Printed through World Print Ltd, Hong Kong

Author's Note
The author wishes to acknowledge the kindness, help
and advice of the following: Roy Millem, Jack
Jenkinson, L. V. Archer, and all his friends at the
Oxford Military Modelling Society. Special gratitude
to his long-suffering wife Pauline, and to John and
Celia Crook. Many of the photographs used in this
book were taken by John Crook.

Readers may find certain subjects touched upon in
this book easier to appreciate if taken in conjunction
with Men-at-Arms 111, *The Armies of Crécy and
Poitiers*; in particular, the earlier title contains several
near-contemporary paintings of battle scenes which
are highly relevant to the Agincourt period.

Introduction

Henry V became King of England in 1413. He was one of the great warrior kings of the country, cast in the same mould as Edward I and Edward III. He was just, pious, athletic, chivalrous, acquisitive, ruthless and eager to gain honour on the field of battle. In many senses he comes closer to an archetype of the better kind of medieval Christian king than any other ruler of the period.

On his accession to the throne Henry set about the vital task of uniting his kingdom. England was tired and divided, its population weary of the continuous feuding which had racked the country for many years. Henry hoped that a successful campaign against the nation's traditional enemy would draw the people together and establish the popularity of the Lancastrian dynasty. He, like many other medieval rulers, also required a military diversion for his barons and it was desirable that their battleground should be on French territory rather than his own.

The political etiquette of the times forbad Henry merely to declare war on France and land an expeditionary force upon her soil. He had first to go through the formal procedure of making apparently reasonable demands on his enemy; but with the diversionary adventure of war never far from his mind, he made these demands so outrageous that it was impossible for France to accept them. They consisted primarily of the crown of France, the whole former Angevin Empire, the Duchy of Normandy, half of Provence, the unpaid ransom of King Jean II (captured at Poitiers), the hand of the French king's daughter and a dowry of two million French crowns. While the representatives of France desperately struggled to find a level of acceptability in these demands, Henry allowed diplomacy to run its course and quietly prepared for war.

For France, Henry's demands could not have been made at a worse time. After the long period of social upheaval which followed Poitiers in 1356, France had begun to recover some semblance of national unity under Charles 'the Wise', but this

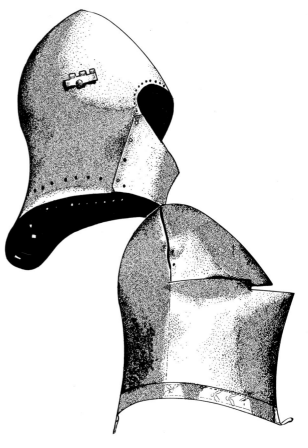

(Top) A 'great bascinet' with skull and neck drawn out of a single piece of metal, and an added lower face plate. This example, which came to light in the Sudan, retains the hinge for a visor. Almost indistinguishable from a 'great helm', this type of helmet gave excellent protection but reduced vision and freedom. (Bottom) The helm from Henry V's funeral achievements in Westminster Abbey, traditionally supposed to have been worn by him at Agincourt and to have suffered the visible damage in combat. Although this is a very early tradition, perhaps dating back to Henry's lifetime, we cannot be certain of its veracity. Note the attachment points at front and rear centre, for buckling to a deep gorget. This would render the helmet immovable, but the head, presumably in a closer-fitting bascinet, would be capable of limited movement inside it.

Tomb effigy of Michael de la Pole, Earl of Suffolk, who died of disease at Harfleur. The wooden effigy shows the pointed form of the bascinet, the crested 'great helm' or tilting helm on which the head rests, and the baviére or 'bevor' of plate attached to the bascinet.

of sanity the French king's sympathies lay with the Armagnacs.

In the early months of 1415 negotiations between France and England broke down, and France, divided and weakened by internal strife and ruled by a pathetic, ageing and frequently mad king, faced yet another expeditionary force from across the Channel.

The Campaign

Henry gathered his huge invasion fleet in the Solent. He used the hundreds of small inlets and tiny creeks along the Hampshire coast to protect and prepare his ships for the Channel crossing. It had taken many months of searching before enough suitable vessels had been purchased or pressed into service, but by 10 August 1415 the task had been completed, and when the king's ship hoisted its mainsail to half-mast the great armada of tiny ships began to manoeuvre slowly into position. On the following day they set sail for France.

The fleet's departure must have been a magnificent spectacle, with the wind filling the embroidered sails and streaming pennons and banners at every masthead. Along the sides of ships the troops had slung heraldic shields and small flags. Musicians blew trumpets and beat drums, and the decks were packed with cheering men and all the impedimenta of war.

Henry sailed in the *Trinité Royale*, the finest and, at 500 tons, the largest ship in the navy. At his masthead he flew the woven banner displaying the three persons of the Godhead and Our Lady, and the arms of St Edward, St George and England. Clustered around the *Trinité Royale* were the other major ships of the fleet, the *Katherine de la Toure*, the *Petite Trinité de la Toure* and the *Rude Coq de la Toure*.

Landfall was made on 13 August. The first sight of France was the long chalk headland of the Seine estuary about three miles west of the small town of Chef de Caux. The English soldiers, with their characteristic blend of ignorance and humour, christened the town 'Kidcox', and some, no doubt, made more of it than that.

Anchors were dropped in the evening but the

had degenerated into total anarchy under his son Charles 'the Mad'. This tragic figure had inherited the throne of France when he was 11, and as he grew older he suffered from increasingly frequent attacks of insanity. For much of the time he was strapped to his bed, while all around him the great magnates and various factions within the kingdom fought each other for power in the court and government.

Of these factions two predominated—the House of Burgundy and the House of Armagnac. At the head of the Armagnac was Charles, Duke of Orleans, the king's nephew and a son-in-law of Count Bernard of Armagnac, who gave his name to the faction. The head of the opposing party was John 'the Fearless', Duke of Burgundy, cousin of Charles of Orleans, and by his inheritance from his mother, Count of Flanders. In his short periods army did not begin disembarking immediately. There was too great a risk that a large proportion of the troops would disappear into the night in search of plunder and then be unable to find their units on the following morning. Instead Henry summoned his senior commanders, consisting of three dukes—York, the king's cousin, Clarence and Gloucester, his brothers—eight earls, two bishops and 19 barons. Between them they agreed that the army should land at dawn; their landing would be preceded by a reconnoitring party led by the knights Sir John Holland, Sir Gilbert Umfraville and Sir John Cornwall, their task being to feel out the enemy's defences and select a suitable place for the army to camp.

So, between the hours of six and seven on the morning of 14 August 1415, hundreds of small boats shuttled back and forth from the ships to the shingle beach. The landing was completed unopposed and by the evening of the same day the troops had begun the construction of a camp near the fortified town of Harfleur.

The siege of Harfleur

The capture of Harfleur was a vital part of Henry's campaign. The facilities of its port would provide a bridgehead for his army, and it was situated at the start of a river route which made Paris easily accessible to Henry's army—a route which took Henry through what he regarded as his own Duchy of Normandy. In the great English military campaigns of the mid-14th century Calais had been the important port. It had the advantage of being close to England, but the disadvantage of being at least 150 miles from Paris, with the barren marshes of Picardy in between.

Harfleur's importance and prosperity was founded on shipping, salt and the weaving industry. Even by the standards of the time it was considered well fortified, and by the French, impregnable. The thick, massive outer wall was about two and a half miles in circumference, with no less than 26 towers situated at strategic points along its length. The three town gates were each a minor fortress with a barbican, drawbridge and

Another view of the De la Pole effigy—note arrangement of plates at shoulder, elbow, and around the face. Protection for the hands is in the form of 'hour glass' gauntlets with raised, decorated gadlings or 'knuckle-dusters'.

portcullis. An important supply of fresh water was guaranteed by the little river Lézarde, which flowed through the centre of the town.

The residents and garrison of Harfleur anticipated Henry's plans and rapidly prepared themselves for a long siege. They promptly flooded the flat land to the north of the town and before they were completely cut off they increased the garrison by 300 or 400 men. They also sent an urgent appeal for relief to the Dauphin, who was assembling an army at Rouen.

The attack on Harfleur gives us an excellent example of medieval siege warfare. The English army surrounded the town and constructed a system of trenches and ramparts around its walls. This was followed by a programme of mining, which failed due to the effectiveness of the French counter-mining activity. Henry brought up great battering rams and numerous stone-slinging machines of various sizes. In retaliation the French resorted to pouring boiling oil and water over their enemies, and their archers shot destructive fire arrows into the protective covering and frames of Henry's siege towers and weapons. They also showered any attackers attempting to climb the walls with quicklime and powdered sulphur. Gunpowder, too, was playing an increasingly important rôle in war. Both sides had primitive cannon. Some of Henry's guns had barrels 12 feet long and calibres of two feet. They could effectively hurl 400- to 500-lb stones over the town walls and through the flimsy roofs of the residents' houses, but their chief function was to smash great breaches in the walls; unfortunately the next morning usually revealed that under cover of darkness the French had filled them up. In time, however, the blast, smoke and regularity of gunfire would wear down the citizens' morale and bring about their surrender. Henry personally supervised the gunnery, frequently spending all night at gun positions preparing the huge pieces for their thrice-daily bombardment.

As the weeks passed, food became short among the besiegers and besieged alike. The unhealthy, marshy air, and hot work in the trenches followed

A beautiful example of a highly decorated armour of plate retaining some mail features: the brass of a knight of the D'Eresby family, c. 1410, in Spilsby Church, Leicestershire.

by damp autumn nights, began to take their toll. This, coupled with a continuous diet of spoilt apples, unripe grapes and large quantities of diseased shellfish washed down with gallons of cider and unfermented wine, led to severe out-breaks of fever and dysentery. Disease ravaged the English army, striking at all levels in the military hierarchy. Bishop Courtney and Michael de la Pole, Earl of Suffolk, were among its most important victims; they and many knights of lower rank and some 2,000 common soldiers died in the filthy encampments around Harfleur. In addition to these serious losses, the king's brother, the Duke of Clarence, the Earl of March, the Earl Marshal, the Earl of Arundel and about 5,000 men were returned home, too sick to continue the campaign. As if all this was not enough, the rate of desertion amongst the English troops increased daily.

On 22 September Harfleur fell, and it was assumed by Henry's war council that the army, weakened by the normal casualties of battle, disease and desertion, would return home to lick its wounds and prepare for a new campaign in the spring of 1416. But Henry would not consider this point of view. He would lead his army on a great *chevauchée*, in the tradition of Edward III and the Black Prince. His banner, quartered with the arms of France and England, would be paraded through the country to signify that he was the true ruler of France. Besides, he claimed that chivalry forbade that he should sneak home without giving his enemy a chance to fight him. In fact Henry's decision was based on far more than mere chivalry. He was an astute politician and a keenly profes-sional soldier, and he knew that if he could tempt the French army into the field he might beat them. He had, after all, the legendary victories of Crécy, Poitiers and Najara to support this theory. He also knew that if he could march through France to Calais unmolested it would add greatly to his prestige and moral ascendancy, and prepare the ground for the next campaign if one was necessary.

The March

A holding force of some 1,200 men were left in Harfleur to guard the town. It was placed under the command of the king's uncle, Thomas Beaufort, Earl of Dorset.

On 8 October the sickly little army of about

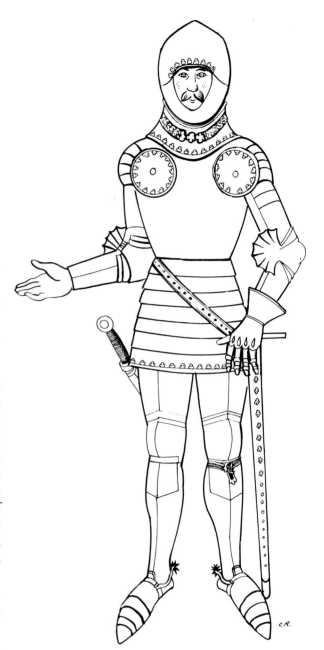

Thomas, Lord Camoys, KG; Trotton, Sussex, 1419. A com-plete suit of plate; the position of the right arm gives us an unusual opportunity to study the arrangement of elbow plates. See Plate B1.

1,000 men-at-arms and 5,000 archers began their 200-mile journey to Calais with rations for eight days. They marched in three divisions, as Edward III's army had done before Crécy in 1346. Commanding the vanguard were Sir John Corn-wall and Sir Gilbert Umfraville; the main body of the army was commanded by the king, and the

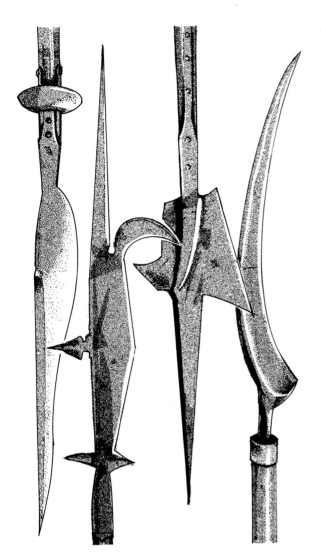

Examples of the many types of pole-arm used for dismounted combat in the early 15th century: (left to right) a glaive, a bill, a halberd and a converted scythe.

rearguard by the Duke of York and the Earl of Oxford.

With a healthy army and perfect weather conditions Henry's change of plan would have been dangerous, even foolhardy; the torrential autumn rains of 1415 and the poor physical condition of the troops made the march seem like a decision verging on insanity. None the less the little army marched steadily on, past Fécamp, over the river Béthune at Arques, and on towards the Somme. Somewhere along its route Henry had to ford the Somme. His first choice was Blanche-taque, where Edward III had crossed over half a century before; but he found the crossing point staked, and on the opposite bank a strong force of French troops waited for him. Henry's scouts searched for other crossing points, but always found the same circumstances. There was no choice for the English army but to painfully wend their way along the southern bank. On 19 October, the tenth day of marching, a crossing was made close to the source of the Somme. Here two fords had been found, one at Béthencourt and the other at Voyennes, but both required some repairs.

The fittest troops, personally supervised by the king, spent all day strengthening the causeway with wood, fascines and straw. Then the army crossed at one ford, the king again controlling this operation, and the baggage and horses crossed at the other under the supervision of Umfraville and Cornwall. As the dispirited troops waded through the cold water, the archers with their bows and arrows above their heads, a strong contingent of French cavalry approached, held their distance and then rode off. On 20 October Henry allowed his men to rest at the small village of Monchy-Lagache, which was situated on the high ground on the northern bank of the Somme.

In the period since the English had landed in France the French had not been inactive. While Harfleur was under siege the Dauphin and the French king began to assemble their army. Most of the great feudatories and their military vassals were summoned to arms. However, the king considered it wiser not to call upon the services of Charles of Orleans and John, Duke of Burgundy. He feared that the acrimony that existed between them would divide the royal army. Instead, he ordered each of them to send 500 men-at-arms. However, Charles flouted his royal master's instructions and appeared in person. Before leaving home he purchased a new suit of armour and a charger and, having paid the men-at-arms and archers in his retinue in advance, he made the 250-mile journey to Rouen to join the swelling ranks of the French army. Here he found the Dukes of Berry, Alençon and Bourbon and the Constable d'Albret. Later they were joined by the Duke of Anjou and Marshal Boucicaut.

As soon as the army at Rouen learned of Henry's movements after leaving Harfleur, an advance force was despatched under Marshal Boucicaut and the Constable d'Albret to prevent Henry crossing the Somme. Alençon, Vendôme and Richemont also rode with this contingent. They travelled quickly and on a more southerly route than Henry, and arrived at the Somme three days before the English.

The main body of the French army left Rouen shortly after the advance force, under the joint command of the Dukes of Orleans and Bourbon. They marched through the countryside along a still more southerly route, hoping to intercept the English army at Amiens; but, arriving on the 17th, they missed them. The English were at that time making their way down the southern bank of the Somme towards their eventual crossing point. The French now turned north to Peronne and waited there. When the English arrived at Monchy-Lagache the two armies were only about six miles apart.

A battle between the two protagonists was now virtually inevitable. Only the time and the place remained undecided.

The French commanders, true to form, now engaged in acrimonious discussion about how they were going to defeat this ragged little force of men. Constable d'Albret, the senior French commander, and the Marshal Boucicaut wisely advised caution: perhaps they alone had remembered the lessons of Crécy and Poitiers. The French army was now firmly astride the route to Calais, the only place where Henry could find safety, so Henry would have to engage the French army before being able to continue towards his goal. The constable was in the position to choose the time and place of the coming battle, and if the French were prepared to wait they might

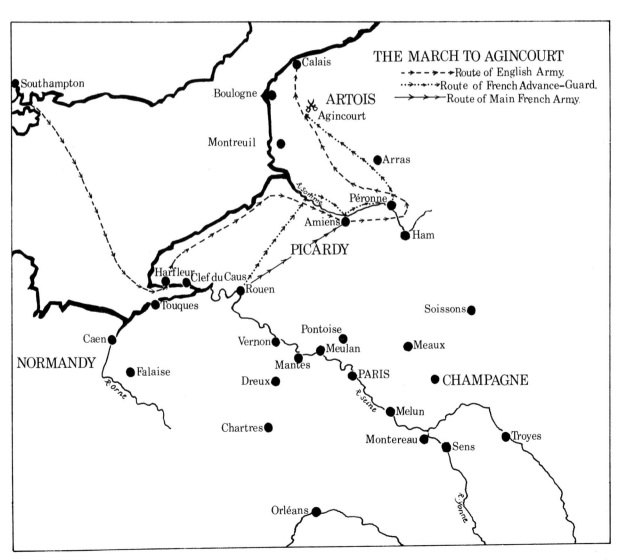

THE MARCH TO AGINCOURT
- – ► – – ► – ►Route of English Army.
··· ► ··· ► ···►Route of French Advance-Guard.
——— ► ——— ► ———Route of Main French Army.

Contemporary drawings of crossbowmen; note the falchion-style swords, the variety of helmet types, the bolts stuck in the belt, and the windlass.

eventually starve the English into submission. Opposed to this apparently negative attitude were the Dukes of Orleans and Bourbon, who were for an immediate attack. To them it was totally unacceptable that this tiny force should be allowed to dictate the manoeuvres of their magnificent army. Their view was supported by the Duke of Berry, who came with the influential contingent of the best French cavalry in his retinue. So d'Albret weakly gave way to his unruly war council, and the heralds were ordered to go to the English camp and declare the French intentions.

Henry was informed that it was known by the French that he had come to conquer their country and depopulate their cities, and the French were now prepared to fight him where and whenever he wished. Henry, with a greater show of confidence than he felt, dismissed their statement, and replied that he did not seek battle; he would march at his own pace straight to Calais, and the French would impede his journey at their own peril. He then rewarded their heralds with gold and returned them to their masters.

Henry's apparent arrogance belied his true feelings. His army was in a desperate state. They had marched for days with little rest. The men were dispirited, cold, wet and exhausted. Many were still suffering from the dysentery they had contracted at Harfleur. They had had no bread for three days, their only food being meat, eked out by small amounts of corn, nuts and vegetables from the fields. To remain in their present position would have resulted in the slow disintegration of the army through sickness and starvation. But the French did precisely what Henry must have prayed for: they gave up what would have been their ultimate advantage of denying Henry the opportunity to fight at his convenience.

As the heralds returned to the French lines Henry put on his embroidered surcoat and ordered his men to do the same. From then on they must be prepared for battle at any moment.

On the following morning, in heavy rain, the English armies continued their weary march northwards. As they passed through Peronne they were surprised to find that the French troops had withdrawn, and their spirits must have lifted a little, only to be dashed by the sight that met them a mile or so out of the town where the road branched off to Bapaume. Here they observed from the churned-up state of the muddy fields that thousands of marching horses and soldiers had passed that way recently. The king's chaplain, Thomas Eltham, poignantly expressed the feelings of the common soldier: 'We who are the rest of the people, raised our hearts and eyes to heaven, crying for God to have compassion upon us, and to turn away from us the power of the French.'

After this ominous sight the English marched for a further three days without making contact with the enemy; but on the morning of the 24th

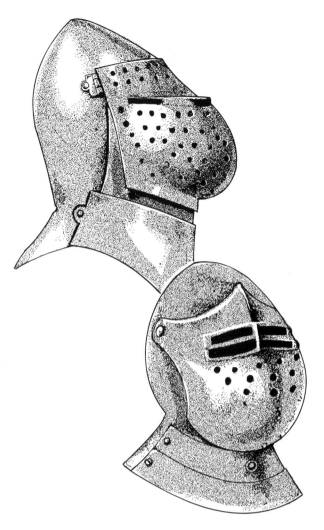

15th century bascinets, showing the more globular forms adopted for both visor and skull, and the additional lower face and neck defences.

one of Henry's advance patrols topped the high ridge at Blagny, near the little river Ternoise, and saw for the first time the glittering splendour of the massive French army moving across the valley below them, completely blocking their route to Calais and safety.

That night the English army rested in the village of Maisoncelle. The men-at-arms probably found shelter in the group of tiny houses in the hamlet, while the archers attempted to find cover in the gardens, orchards and woods. Most of the English soldiers must have regarded that night as their last on earth, so they prayed, confessed their sins and made their peace with God. Faced with the inevitable, most would have sharpened their weapons, and prepared themselves for the morn-

Henry V, as shown on the counterseal of the Gold Seal, 1415. Note the crest, displayed not only on the helm but on the horse's head too. The arms are Quarterly, France Modern and England—see Plate B2.

ing, before falling into a more or less fitful sleep under the chilling rain.

In the French camp, in and around the villages of Tramecourt and Agincourt, the atmosphere was very different; confident of easy victory they drank and diced over the important prisoners they expected to take. A cart was painted and decorated in which to drag Henry, as the most illustrious captive, through the streets of Rouen. Food was cooked over camp fires. Straw was fetched for the nobles' beds, and the horses were exercised to keep them warm on a rainy autumn night.

The Armies

The French was by far the larger of the two armies present at Agincourt, but it is difficult, if not impossible, to establish the exact size. The estimates of contemporary chroniclers range from 10,000 to 150,000 or more. Lt.Col. Burne in his book *The Agincourt War* convincingly computes that there were between 20,000 and 30,000 men under the French banner. But as the medieval historians were not good at such calculations the final figure will never be known: recorded figures were selected more for dramatic effect than for scholarly accuracy.

As much as 60 per cent of the French army were men-at-arms; the remainder were trained garrison troops drawn from France's larger towns and castles, with some mercenaries from the northern Italian cities, and the feudal levies. The French commanders were obviously confident that they had sufficient men to defeat the English, because we find the Constable d'Albret rejecting an offer of 6,000 crossbowmen from the city militia of Paris.

There is little argument about the size of the English army: most of the contemporary chroniclers record its size as 6,000, of whom 1,000 were men-at-arms and the remainder archers.

* * *

As the dawn broke cold and wet on 25 October 1415, the two armies began to draw themselves up in their battle positions.

The French placed themselves between Tramecourt on their left flank and Agincourt on their right flank, their formations firmly blocking the English army's route to Calais. Their front was restricted to about three-quarters of a mile by the woods which fringed the two villages. The troops were marshalled into three massive divisions, one behind the other. The first two divisions were dismounted men-at-arms; at either end of these two divisions waited the heavily armoured cavalry, and to the front of the first division were large numbers of crossbowmen and archers.

The French intended to open the engagement by showering the English archers with bolts and arrows; situated on the flanks of the most forward division were some primitive guns which were also intended to add their missiles to this opening barrage. After the English archers were neutralised the flanking cavalry were to charge forward and trample them underhoof. While these two happy events occurred the first two French divisions of dismounted men-at-arms were to advance steadily and engage the English men-at-arms, and by their overwhelming superiority of numbers defeat them. The French third and rear division was kept as a reserve, and was there to deal with any survivors who might attempt to escape from the field of battle.

Even with the advantage of hindsight this strategy seemed sound, and it should have proved successful; but it did not take into consideration the irrational, competitive pride of the French nobility. The honour of standing in the front rank was so important that these nobles elbowed and jostled the archers and crossbowmen aside until most of them stood uselessly behind the cavalry and the first division of the men-at-arms. Not only were the lowborn archers and crossbowmen ordered to the rear, but so too were the nobles and knights of lower rank and hundreds of pages and squires. When the French army finally settled itself for the 'opening' of the battle there were 12 princes of the blood in the front rank, and in the first two divisions there were thousands of dukes, counts, barons and knights of high birth, many of them bearing the distinguished family names borne by their fathers and grandfathers at Crécy and Poitiers. The chroniclers tell us that there were so many banners fluttering above the first division that there seemed to be more there than in the whole English army, and after considerable argument some had to be furled and carried to the rear.

Following yet more argument the command of the first French division was shared between the Constable d'Albret, Marshal Boucicaut and the Dukes of Orleans and Bourbon; with them stood the Counts d'Eu and Richemont.

The second division, thought to be twice as large as the first, was under the command of the Dukes of Bar and Alençon. The Counts of Nevers, Vaudemont, Blamont, Salines, Grandpré and Roussy also stood in its ranks.

The third division was placed as much as half a mile to the rear of the two forward divisions, somewhere near the village of Ruisseauville. This division consisted almost entirely of mounted men and was possibly the largest body of French troops present. Many of them were Gascons, Bretons and Poitevins. The division was under the command of the Counts of Marle, Dampmartin, Fauquembergh and the Lord Lenroy. Not surprisingly the troops in this division were of lower social standing than the remainder of the French army, with only its commanders being of noble blood.

On the French right wing, close up against the edge of the woods, were about 1600 men-at-arms whose function was to attack the English flank. On the other wing were 800 dismounted horsemen led by the revered Sir Clignet de Brabant, who were to break the English line. Scattered around the two flanks were also groups of archers commanded by the Lord Rambures, master of the crossbows. Here too were an assortment of ineffectual cannon and perhaps some siege engines, their gunners cursing the tightly packed, restless troops who obscured their target.

Henry rose early that morning and immediately after Mass put on his embroidered surcoat, which was quartered with the arms of France and England. Wearing his crown on his bascinet he rode a small grey horse to where his army was being marshalled into its fighting formation.

Henry's men-at-arms stood in three small divisions and consisted of about 990 men in total. Between the men-at-arms stood wedge-shaped groups of archers. On either wing and curving slightly forwards, thus making the whole line slightly concave, were more archers. Their task was to provide fire from the sides and front. The right wing was commanded by the Duke of York, the left by Thomas, Lord Camoys (Plate B1) and the king (Plate B2) commanded the centre. The English army stood in a field of young corn, not

Plan of the battle of Agincourt, 25 October 1415.

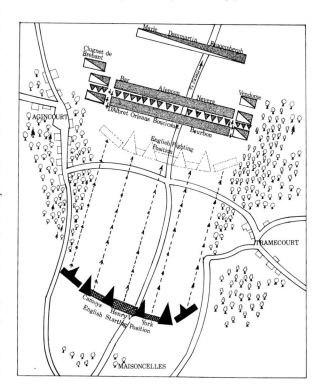

far in front of the village of Maisoncelles, with a very gentle slope running away from them and rising slightly towards the French. The distance between the two waiting armies was about three-quarters of a mile.

The English baggage carts, priests and sick were left in Maisoncelle under the guard of ten men-at-arms and some 20 archers. Henry had ordered the priests to pray hard for an English victory.

With the English army now in position, uneasily awaiting the coming onslaught, the 28-year-old king addressed his men. He stressed the justice of his conquest of France; exhorted them with their responsibility to their families back home in England; and reminded them that every archer

The head and upper limbs of the effigy of Lord Bardolf in St Mary's Church, Dennington, Suffolk; see Plate B3. Note the large gorget, the jewelled orle, and the Lancastrian Household collar, frequently in evidence on effigies and brasses of the period.

who allowed himself to be captured would probably have three fingers hacked off his right hand so that he could not draw a bow in the service of his king again.

The Battle

The two armies now faced each other, but some hours were to pass before battle was joined. During this period negotiations were re-opened in an attempt to establish a truce. The French conditions required Henry to renounce his claim to the throne of France and to surrender Harfleur. In return he would be allowed to keep the territories that he held in Guienne and Picardy. Despite his desperate circumstances Henry rejected these conditions and stood by his original claims made in England before the campaign began. The French messengers returned to their commanders,

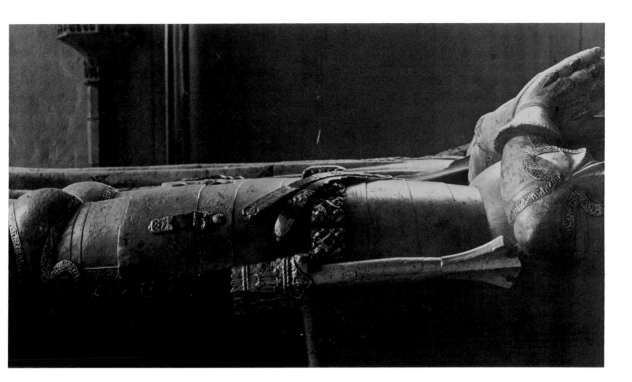

and the two armies settled themselves once more to wait.

As the hours passed slowly by, Henry realised he must provoke the French army into attacking him, or his weary troops would start to collapse from hunger and sickness before they came to grips with the French; it is even possible that this was the French intention. Henry's only chance lay in a strategy which would draw the French into the devastating fire of the English archers. At 11 a.m. Henry could wait no longer and called for the distinguished marshal of the army, Sir Thomas Erpingham (Plate E2), to bring the archers into position. The ageing, grey-haired knight rode in front of the archers and packed them closer together in the arrowhead formations in which they fought so well. With the archers ready, he tossed his baton of rank into the air and cried 'Nestrocque!' (thought to mean 'Now strike!' or 'Knee! Stretch!'); this signified that he now regarded the army as ready for battle. Sir Thomas's order was answered by a great shout which echoed up and down the English ranks. His task completed, Sir Thomas dismounted and returned to his place near the king, his large green and white banner fluttering beside him. The army was then silent for a few minutes, the tension growing with every second; then Henry shouted the orders that all his

Detail from the Bardolf effigy showing the rich brass edge-decoration on the plates, the straps on the lower taces, the diagonal and horizontal belts, and the typical early 15th century hand-and-a-half sword.

men had waited for so long: 'Banners advance! In the name of Jesus, Mary and St George!'

Spontaneously the whole army knelt, drew the sign of the cross on the ground, bent and kissed the earth and took a piece of soil in their mouths; then they stood, and began their long march across the waterlogged field. They were slow but resolute. Twice they halted, allowing the heavily armoured men-at-arms to regain their breath and the archers, out on each flank of the army, to maintain their position. As they came on, drums were beaten and trumpets sounded, and added to this was the continuous shouting of the battle cry 'St George! St George!'

The sight of the ragged lines of English soldiers advancing towards them threw the French into total confusion. They had waited, secure in the knowledge that they would control the pace of the battle; now, seeing that his army might have lost the initiative, Constable d'Albret ordered his men to confess their sins, attack the English and fight bravely.

When they were within 200 yards of the first French division the English halted, and the archers

Lower limbs of the Bardolf effigy; note spur-straps, and the insignia of the Order of the Garter round the left leg below the knee.

hammered into the soft earth the wooden sharpened stakes which they had dragged over the long, weary miles from the Somme. This task completed, they retired behind their pointed screen and began to pour their deadly arrows into the closely packed ranks of Frenchmen.

From the French right flank the heavy cavalry, under Sir William de Saveuses, lumbered forward; their inevitably slow attack was reduced to a funeral pace by the clinging mud of the churned-up ground. As they squelched forward the French knights hunched themselves low in the saddle and bent their heads forward to deflect the hail of arrows falling upon them.

The French made their point of impact the English left flank, but the archers here, with their ranks close against the Agincourt wood, gave no ground and made it impossible for the French cavalry to ride down their line. Quickly the whole attack was reduced to a frontal assault, but those knights who survived the showers of arrows could not force their way through the wall of stakes. Many horses, thrust forward by the momentum of

those behind them or maddened by the numerous arrows that pierced their flesh, were forced onto the stakes and impaled, their riders being quickly despatched by the archers—among them their leader, de Saveuses.

Within a short time the cavalry had been repulsed. A few survivors turned their horses and rode back to the French lines, smashing aside the heavily armoured men-at-arms in the first and second French divisions. A small body of cavalry under Sir Clignet de Brabant had left the main attack and found their way to the English baggage carts, which they promptly plundered.

Now the massive French first division walked ponderously forward, the convex glancing surfaces of their helmets and shoulders bent towards their enemy. For the first 50 yards or so they moved in line abreast, but as the arrows began to thin their ranks they formed themselves into columns. This only provided protection for a short time; soon the crossfire from the archers on the outer fringes of the concave formation and the narrowing of the space between the two woods forced the French men-at-arms closer together, eventually packing them shoulder to shoulder once more. On they came, soaked with sweat and gasping for air inside their steel shells, each step an immense physical effort in the churned quagmire left by the cavalry. Slowly they stumbled towards the points in the line where the English men-at-arms waited. If honour was to be satisfied the French men-at-arms must have personal combat with English men-at-arms; the low-born bowmen had to be ignored.

As the French closed on the English it was necessary to quicken the pace so that the momentum created by their weight and forward thrust would enable them to smash their way deeply into the English ranks, and this they did, driving the English line back some 12 feet at their point of impact. But this initial success could not be exploited; the French were now so closely packed that many of them could not lift their arms above their waists, and since their visors were down there was little chance of striking accurately at an enemy in the flailing mass of armoured limbs and weapons. Worse still, the sheer pressure from the rear of the first French division was forcing those at the front off their feet, and being unable to rise again they were trampled into the mud by their own comrades.

The English recovered quickly from that first moment of impact and took full advantage of the appalling confusion before them. Soon they were killing large numbers of the tightly packed Frenchmen with comparative ease. The archers too, their hunger and exhaustion forgotten, flung down their bows and arrows and taking their swords, clubs and axes eagerly launched themselves into the slaughter. Many grabbed discarded weapons which lay about them, the great maces, long swords and lethal war hammers. With unrestricted agility and wicked determination they knocked the French knights off their feet and then hacked their way through the vulnerable joints in their armour. Some, kneeling astride the fallen, thrashing figures, were seen to hammer the needle-sharp 'daggers of mercy' through the visor slits. However, many of the French were not killed by the English at all, but suffocated or drowned, trapped in their armour, in the liquid mud beneath the weight of their fellows.

The dead, wounded and dying lay in great piles along the battlefront; sometimes the archers would climb on them, to leap into some closely packed group of the enemy. In the meantime some of their comrades kept up a deadly hail of arrows on the advancing second French division. It would be misleading to imagine the battle was easy for the English. In the mass of flailing arms the fat Duke of York was hurled to the ground and crushed or asphyxiated to death. Near him Henry was beaten to his knees several times; on one occasion his brilliant crown was nearly hacked from his helmet by a French axe which removed a fleuron on its journey, and three of Henry's Welsh esquires were killed at his side.

Seeing that the battle had begun to go hopelessly wrong the knights in the second French division began to drift away from the field. The Dukes of Alençon and Bar, who, it will be remembered, were in command, pleaded with them to stay; but having failed, they returned to the fighting, where it is said d'Alençon wounded the Duke of Gloucester. D'Alençon was immediately overpowered by the king's bodyguard, and as he raised his hand to surrender, an English soldier, caught in the frenzied excitement of killing, struck the duke a great blow from his

English banners, about four feet square, were carried by lords and bannerets. Those shown here were carried in Henry V's division at Agincourt. (Top) The Royal Arms of England, in gold on red and blue. (Centre) The Lancastrian family badge of a fox-tail slung from a blue and white staff. (Bottom) The red cross of St George on a white field.

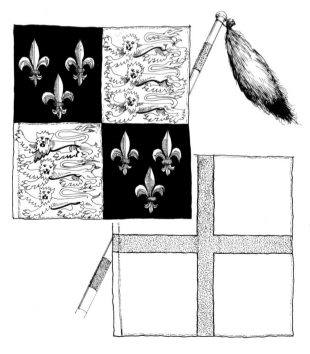

battle-axe and killed him instantly.

The Duke of Brabant, youngest brother of John the Fearless, Duke of Burgundy, arrived late in the battle. He had ridden so hard and fast from a family wedding in the north that he had outstripped most of his retinue and arrived at Agincourt without armour or weapons, so he borrowed the armour of his chamberlain, Goblet Vosken, and wore one of his trumpet banners as his heraldic surcoat. Siezing a discarded weapon he rode into the mêlée, and was slain.

After two or three hours the intensity of the fighting began to decline, until eventually it was safe for the English to begin sorting their prisoners They pulled the living from the piles of dead, rejected and despatched the badly wounded, and soon large groups of unarmed prisoners of ransomable quality stood waiting to begin the long march to Calais. In fact there were so many prisoners that they outnumbered all the survivors in the English army.

Meanwhile the whole third French division, which had waited and watched the horrific spectacle of their greatest nobles and champions being slaughtered, began to melt away from the scene. Passing through the Tramécourt woods, they looked as though they intended to attack the English from the rear. This manoeuvre thoroughly alarmed the English and, to add to the confusion, three French nobles and some of the peasant levy attacked the English baggage carts again. Henry, fearing that these two factions might unite and, even at this late stage in the battle, might snatch victory from the English, ordered the deaths of all

There were many different types of flag used in medieval warfare. The standard, a long, tapering flag with rounded ends, displayed the owner's full arms, and acted as a rallying point in battle. Both these examples are known to have been used as personal standards by Henry V. (Top) Red and white cross of St George in the hoist; the fly divided horizontally, white over blue, crossed with the motto 'Dieu et Mon Droit' ('God and My Right') in gold lettering on gold-bordered white strips, and charged with the swan of Bohun in white with gold collar and chain, and the gold tree stumps of Woodstock. (Bottom) The same as the above but charged with the white antelope and the red roses of Lancaster.

the prisoners: he simply did not have the manpower to guard large numbers of able-bodied enemy, surrounded by discarded weapons, if he was to hold off another attack simultaneously. The English knights were horrified: not, one hastens to add, for humanitarian reasons, but because of the vast sums of ransom money that would be lost. Nevertheless, with the aid of 200 archers, innumerable French men-at-arms were quickly put to death. The vast proportion of them, who were in armour but had removed their helmets, had their heads hacked off.

By the time night closed in around Agincourt the English troops had completed the task of stripping the corpses of their armour, and the flower of French chivalry and thousands of knights of lower rank lay naked and dead on the desolate, muddy field. Amongst them lay the Dukes of Alençon, Bar and Brabant, and the Constable Charles d'Albret. Altogether it is estimated that between 7,000 and 10,000 Frenchmen died at Agincourt on that day. In addition to these losses there were some 1,500 surviving prisoners, among them the Duke of Bourbon, the Counts of Eu, Vendôme and Richemont, Marshal Boucicaut and most illustrious of all, Charles, Duke of Orleans.

By comparison the English casualties were very low, perhaps 500 being the highest estimate. The most notable deaths being those of the Duke of York and the young Earl of Suffolk, whose father had died of dysentery at Harfleur. Also listed amongst the English dead were Sir Richard Kyghley, Sir Thomas Fitzhenry, Sir John de Peniton, Sir Walter Lord, and Dafydd ap Llewelyn ap Hywel, known as David Gamme, the latter being knighted by Henry a few hours before he finally died of wounds.

On the following day Henry and his victorious army continued the last 45 miles of their march to Calais, taking with them their spoils of war and their important captives. Two of their prisoners, Marshal Boucicaut and the Duke of Bourbon, were to die in England, their families being unable to meet Henry's massive ransom demands. Charles, Duke of Orleans remained in England until 1436 and was only released on the payment of 240,000 ecús and the promise not to bear arms against England again.

Painting of a knight from a manuscript believed to have been illustrated in France in c.1410. The style of armour is late 14th century: pig-faced bascinet with camail; plate armour over the outer surfaces of the limbs and mail beneath it protecting the inner surfaces; and tight, short jupon concealing the torso defences.

Command

As a general rule the commander-in-chief of the medieval army was the leader of the nation, tribal group or clan. Beneath him were the various levels of command, which tended to reflect the hierarchical structure of the society from which the army was drawn. Thus senior positions of command went to the highest ranking members of the nobility, who by virtue of their wealth and station usually brought the largest numbers of troops to the battlefield.

Throughout the period it is customary to find the commander-in-chief on the battlefield, though contrary to general belief he does not often lead his front ranks into battle, or even come into physical

The effigy of the 2nd Earl of Warwick shows the earlier, mid- to late-14th century armour which was probably present in quite large quantities among the lesser members of the armies at Agincourt.

contact with the enemy. He is more often found with the reserves, leaving the immediate tactical development of the action to able subordinates. From the 11th century through to the end of the Hundred Years War we have numerous examples of this characteristic. At Crécy in 1346 Edward III, who was commander-in-chief, left the fighting to his senior commanders Warwick, Oxford, Northampton, Arundel and others, while he watched the battle from slightly to the rear in the reserve. His opponent Philip de Valois, King of France, fought in the battle and was wounded, but only after the initial attacks on the English position had failed and most of his army had been committed.

At Poitiers in 1356, Prince Edward, the Prince of Wales, was in command of the English army, and we find him in the reserves while his senior officers are involved in the fighting. The commander of the French army, Jean II, is also in his reserve division, and once more becomes involved only after his first division has been defeated and the second of his three divisions has left the field.

Agincourt is the exception to the rule. The French king was not present at the battle; instead the French command seems to have been shared between the Constable Charles d'Albret and the Dukes of Orleans and Bourbon. The constable should have been the senior commander, but his views before the battle seem to have been ignored, and he appears to have been unable to exert any authority over the situation. The English army was too small to have enough troops to form a reserve and Henry, the commander, was so closely involved in battle that he was beaten to the ground several times and his crown nearly hacked from his helmet. The senior French commanders and their subordinates were so eager to share in the destruction of the tiny English army that they foolishly placed themselves in the first two divisions.

Throughout the whole of the Hundred Years War we see this fascinating contrast between the senior commanders of France and England revealing itself. The English for some unaccountable reason produced strong commanders-in-chief. The Earl of Northampton, Edward III, Edward, Prince of Wales and Henry V were all competent and masterful, unwilling to endure opposition and given to making firm, clear decisions. As a consequence they were generally well liked and respected by their men. All these men gave their subordinate commanders areas of responsibility in battle and expected these to be seen through. Although they respected the code of chivalry of the age, they did not allow it to take priority over a good chain of command, sound strategy and effective military administration. Sadly, the French were always cursed with weak commanders-in-chief, and the very nature of their deeply divided society inevitably resulted in disloyal and irresponsible subordinate commanders.

The French had the additional handicap of certain nobles holding important military positions within the army—the offices of constable and marshal—without necessarily being able to command an appropriate obedience.

The word 'constable' stems from 'count of the stable'. It was an appointment which involved varying sorts of responsibilities through the ages. In England from the reign of King Stephen the Lord High Constable was the quartermaster-general of the court and army. He did not usually have overall command of the army and when this did occur it was usually because that specific constable was a noble of high rank and not through his military office. Under the three Edwards the constable's duties became the maintenance of order in the neighbourhood of the court and the protection of the king's household. In the field these duties were extended to include the area of the royal camp. Some time later, when Edward III set up a court of chivalry, it became the duty of the Lord High Constable to preside over enquiries into crimes committed by knights.

In France the constable was given far greater responsibilities and was regarded in a totally different way. He was the first officer of the crown, the chief commander of the army and the authority on all matters concerned with chivalry. In theory he outranked all nobles, even princes of the blood, and was second only to the king.

The other great military office was that of marshal. Through the reigns of the Norman and Plantagenet kings it was an office which commanded great respect. In battle the marshal carried the golden staff and was responsible for the directing and ordering of the troops on the battlefield, and he frequently had the duty of leading troops into action. Another of his duties was to make decisions on matters concerning the rules and practices of chivalry.

The difficulty for the French army lay not in the duties of these officers but in the tendency of the French kings to appoint them from the lower levels of nobility. If we look at the marshals of the French army throughout the period, Guy de Nesle (1348), Arnoul d'Audrehem (1351–68), Jean le Clermont (1352–6), the elder and younger Boucicaut (1368–91), and Louis de Sancerre (1368–97), we find

Two other banners believed to have been carried in Henry's division during the Agincourt campaign. (Top) The banner of the Holy Trinity—gold lettering on white device on red field. (Bottom) The Arms of St Edward the Confessor—gold devices on a dark blue field. This was also carried by Richard II.

Contemporary drawings of archers; both wear helmets, and are probably more fortunate in this respect than most of the bowmen at Agincourt. Note jackets of nailed brigandine work; sword and buckler; and bundles of arrows attached to the belts.

that only de Sancerre came from the high nobility. Perhaps the most outstanding example of this is the appointment of Bertrand du Guesclin as Constable of France from 1370 to 1380. Du Guesclin, although a brilliant professional soldier, was originally little more than a captain of mercenaries.

Froissart was amazed that du Guesclin should bear this illustrious title, since he could barely read or write. So it is inevitable that these men should be considered as inferiors by the touchy and insanely proud senior nobles, and many of the latter abused the great power and status derived through their social rank. Not surprisingly this sometimes led to an inability on the part of the French war councils to agree on strategy right up until the moment before the battle opened. At Crécy we have disagreement before the first attack. At Poitiers the Marshals Clermont and Audreham were not only unable to agree with the other members of the war council but argued with each other even as they rode into battle. At Agincourt we have the wise advice of Charles

d'Albret, the army commander, to contain the English army but not to attack them, being completely ignored. It is certain that this constant conflict amongst the senior French commanders contributed towards the major defeats of the French army throughout the Hundred Years War.

Organization in the field

The typical army formation of the Hundred Years War consisted of three divisions or *batailles*. Occasionally this formation was increased by two wings, sometimes of cavalry, but more often of archers or crossbowmen. Although this way of organizing the army seems complex, it is simplified if we remember that these divisions would attack the enemy one after the other and not simultaneously.

The soldiers serving in each division were frequently not merely grouped together at the beginning of each impending battle, but were raised in the same geographical area and often served together throughout a complete campaign, usually under the same commander. Many of these units were raised considerable distances away from the area where they campaigned, the troops being sub-tenants or tenants of their lord, who became their commander in the field. But this was not always the case: sometimes, on arrival at the marshalling point before the battle opened, the constable or marshal selected individual groups of soldiers to serve, for example, in the vanguard or rear division, or certain troops might be used as infantry although they had arrived expecting to participate in the action as cavalry.

Each division was composed of groups of soldiers, fighting under a banner or pennon. The size of these units generally depended on the size of the division as a whole. The unit commanders held the rank of knight banneret or knight batchelor. A knight batchelor had won his spurs but did not own land, or he was a young knight serving in the entourage of a banneret. The knight banneret was usually a knight promoted or selected for military skills, and to some degree for his wealth and land; as a result of this he could lead men into battle under his own banner. It was not at all uncommon for a knight batchelor to be promoted on the field of battle; the tail of his pennon was then symbolically cut off to make the rectangular banner of his new rank.

As the years of the war dragged on, the kings of France attempted to improve their army by issuing royal ordinances. Put simply, some of these declared that military service was a trade, and required payment. These rates in 1351 were as follows: 40 sous a day for a banneret, 20 sous for a knight, 10 for a squire, 5 for a valet, 3 for an infantryman, $2\frac{1}{2}$ for an armour bearer or similar attendant. Every man in the army was also required to be subordinate to a commander and to take an oath to him not to leave the commander's unit without an order. This was an attempt to avoid the crippling problem of the feudal barons using their right to independently leave the campaign whenever they had completed their period of obligation. There was also a percentage payment for some officers based on the number of men under their command.

One ordinance attempted to deal with the many men who did not come under the command of any officer, but arrived and fought as independent troops; these were to be organized into *compagnies*, *routes* or *banniers* (different names for the same groupings) of between 25 and 80 men and placed under the command of a banneret. Any troops who arrived in groups of less than 25 were to be given into the command of a knight batchelor or even an esquire. A later ordinance decreed that the size of these *routes*, *compagnies* or *banniers* should be increased to a hundred men and only commanded by senior officers commissioned by the king.

Cavalry

The mounted section of the army consisted of men-at-arms on large horses, although there was a form of light cavalry known as hobilars on both sides. The term 'men-at-arms' is a loose and imprecise way of describing an armoured fighting man; this term encompassed in its meaning kings, nobles, knights banneret, knights batchelor, and esquires or sergeants. Thus all knights are men-at-arms, but not all men-at-arms are knights.

Despite the magnificent splendour of medieval cavalry and its social importance to men of high birth, its achievements on the field of battle rarely amounted to more than breaking into the enemy ranks. This was achieved by packing hundreds of the heavily armoured, mounted men in tight formations and then unleashing them on the enemy. The momentum created by weight, speed and force was intended to drive a wedge into the enemy formations which could then be exploited. Sometimes the sight and sound of charging cavalry would induce inexperienced infantry to break ranks and run. However, when using the term 'charge', we must remember that it is unlikely that mass formations of medieval cavalry ever reached speeds faster than a trot, and at Agincourt the clinging morass through which the French cavalry had to ride reduced their speed still further; but no doubt the shock and force at the moment of impact still had its effect if the charge was delivered at the right point in the enemy lines.

Having broken into the enemy formation they needed to exploit their advantage, perhaps by riding along the lines or turning the flank; but it was at this point that mounted troops became vulnerable. If they were engaged against confident and experienced infantry they could be absorbed and then isolated and killed at will. To escape this

Another contemporary drawing of crossbowmen, one of them spanning his bow with the aid of a windlass and foot-stirrup. Note long-flighted bolts. The bowmen wear brigandine jackets over chain mail, and (left) some plate protection on the arms and shoulders. Among infantry any armour worn seems normally to have been confined to the upper body and limbs, with occasional use of knee-pieces.

danger the cavalry avoided deep penetration and withdrew for further attacks.

In general medieval cavalry were deployed in large formations, and their lack of training in tactics or manoeuvres gave even the most imaginative commander little choice other than to use his force as a bludgeon. This, coupled with the traditional arrogance and self-conscious courage of the nobility who formed by far the greater part of the cavalry, produced little flexibility and many problems. We have only to examine the actions of the French cavalry at Crécy, Poitiers and Agincourt to find glaring examples of these characteristics. To regard the mounted man-at-arms as merely a lumbering fool on a horse is to underestimate him, however. He was in fact the all-round soldier of the age. He fought dismounted in land and naval engagements; he was deployed on foot to stiffen units of weak or demoralised infantry; he fought dismounted in the many castle and city sieges of the period, frequently taking an active interest in siege engineering and the increasing use of artillery.

Infantry

At Agincourt the quality of the foot soldiers on each side varied considerably. These variations revealed themselves in weapons, armour, numbers and morale.

The French had by far the larger body of infantry, many of whom were common foot soldiers. Although there are no accurate statistics recorded, their numbers probably amounted to as many as 20,000 of the French army. There was little they could do in the major battles of the period other than trail in the wake of the mounted men-at-arms. frequently arriving on the battlefield after the fighting had ended. These were the peasant levies from Picardy, Artois, Normandy and Champagne. They were not trained in the ways of war, and as such were difficult if not impossible to manoeuvre on the battlefield. What armour they possessed was limited to a simple leather jerkin and, if they were fortunate, an iron or leather helmet; their weapons were often merely crude modifications of agricultural implements, simple swords, knives and short bows. Some wore the white cross of St Denis on their jerkins to distinguish them from the general run of

peasants. In action they were frequently used to form mass screens, thus reducing the flexibility of the enemy. They were useful as a labour force in the many city and castle sieges of the period, and also for performing the more menial tasks of camp life.

Apart from the peasant levy, the French had trained infantry in the form of garrison and regular troops armed with various forms of pole-arms such as pikes, halberds and spears. There was an increasing use of crossbow units raised and founded by civic bodies. The French also employed mercenary troops, of which the best were the crossbowmen from the northern Italian cities, particularly Genoa.

The English army had no equivalent to the peasant levy; the long-established practice of obtaining the best troops through selection and paid contract had ensured a reasonably high standard of fitness and military competence. Besides, the limited size of the armies which could be transported across the English Channel meant that only men of a certain quality would be taken.

At Agincourt the most decisive infantry weapon was the longbow, but other weapons used by English footsoldiers were pikes, halberds, spears, clubs and swords. The crossbow did not seem to find favour with English soldiers. There was an ever-increasing use of mounted infantry archers on both sides. Edward III seems to have developed bodies of mounted archers to provide himself with mobile mounted firepower on the field of battle.

Armour

The second half of the 14th century and the first two decades of the 15th were periods of great experimentation in armour and rapid developments in design. It is possibly the period that saw more detail changes in armour than any other. These changes ran virtually parallel in the armies of both protagonists. There was, of course, a wide variety of armour worn on the field of Agincourt, the various types spanning a period of some 150 years; the better armour would be worn by the wealthier knights and the poorer quality or older armour by knights of lower social standing, or even well-equipped sergeants, men-at-arms or esquires.

At the beginning of the 15th century the same defences that were observed in the previous

1. Crossbowman
2. English archer
3. Infantryman

A

1. Thomas, Lord Camoys, KG
2. King Henry V
3. William Phelipp, Lord Bardolph, KG

B

1. English man-at-arms
2. Mountjoy, King of Arms
3. Garter, King of Arms

C

1. Jean le Meingre, dit 'Boucicaut,' Marshal of France
2. Charles d'Albert, Constable of France
3. Charles, Duke of Orleans

1. Richard de Vere, Earl of Oxford
2. Sir Thomas Erpingham, KG
3. Sir Edmund de Thorpe

E

F

1. Hand Gunner
2. Edward, Duke of Bar
3. Artilleryman

1. Mounted archer
2. and 3. Crossbowmen

H

century were generally in use, namely the bascinet; camail and haubergeon of chain mail; breast and back plates; jupon; and plate defences over the arms and legs. But we see emerging around 1410, for the first time, a complete suit of 'white' armour (i.e. bright steel) without any form of textile covering. Until this date the torso had always been covered by the heraldic jupon or surcoat. An early example of this characteristic is seen in the brass of Sir John Wykotes, 1410, at Great Tew, Oxfordshire. This is not to say that the jupon disappeared; we can find ample evidence that it remained in use in England and on the Continent until the 1420s.

Until around 1410 the knight's head, neck and shoulders had been protected by the bascinet, with its mail curtain—camail; but this latter was relatively heavy, with most of the weight being transferred to the top of the head via the helmet. This was gradually replaced by a gorget or deep collar-piece of plate armour: the bascinet was constructed in such a way that it was overlapped by the gorget and could still turn to the right and left, though perhaps less freely than had been the case. The whole weight of the neck defences was thus transferred to the shoulders. The bascinet typically became more globular in form, though it still rose to a pointed apex. Generally it consisted of two halves; the lower half, known as the baviére, was riveted to the upper skull along the temples.

Once the jupon had begun to disappear we see a complete breast and back plate with an attached skirt of five or six taces, or overlapping plates, extending downwards to the mid-thighs; the cuirass sometimes has hinges on the left side and is secured by straps and buckles on the right, as displayed on the brass of Sir Thomas Braunstone, 1401, at Wisbech, Cambridgeshire. For about the first two decades of the 15th century the skirt of the haubergeon could usually be seen beneath the taces, but by 1420 this garment seems to have been discarded and protection came from the plate armour and quilted gambeson alone. To this latter garment pieces of mail were attached to protect those areas not covered by plate; these usually consisted of a standing collar, gussets at the arm-pits and elbow joints, and a skirt of mail, usually just covering the thighs but sometimes, in Italy in particular, extending to the knees.

The shoulders were protected by laminated épaulières; these were short, oblong plates which did not curve completely around the front of the shoulders, and instead plates or roundels of various forms, were worn over the front of the shoulder joints. The upper and lower arm was covered by two curved plates on each part, with visible hinges and fastenings. On the elbows were roundels or beautiful fan-like plates, which increased in size throughout the century. The gauntlets were deeper than those in the preceding century, often having two or three joints in each cuff. The ornamental gadlings remained, often beautifully worked in brass, gilt and even jewels, with some gauntlets even having engraved finger nails.

The legs were protected by cuissarts, genouil-lières, grevières and sollerets which did not differ greatly from those worn before 1400, with one exception: these were small plates worn over the back of the knee joints, which seem to have appeared briefly and then disappeared until the first half of the 16th century.

In the earlier part of the period the sword belt was worn horizontally around the taces with the sword and misericorde attached to it, but gradually this became unfashionable or impractical and was replaced by a narrow belt which passed diagonally across the taces, supporting only the sword on the left hip. This was frequently decorated by trefoils, quatrefoils or some geometric design, but is not often found with a buckle. The misericorde now became attached to one of the plates covering the right hip.

It is useful at this point to mention that the sword had changed slightly from that carried at Crécy and Poitiers, the quillons being straightened and the hilt being elongated, transforming the sword into a 'hand-and-a-half', or 'bastard' sword. Thus, though the sword was generally wielded with one hand, extra force or thrust could be obtained by bringing the other hand up to the pommel.

Shields were beginning to show a marked change during this period. They were usually smaller than those carried in the 14th century and were sometimes notched to accommodate a lance, and became more concave in shape to deflect an opponent's lance. The increasingly complete

The effigy of the Earl of Oxford—see Plate E1—shows the mail camail still worn beneath the plate gorget, and armpit and elbow defences.

protection provided by plate armour led to a decline in the importance of the shield, which would almost disappear among armoured knights as the century progressed.

The Common Soldier

Since there were no fixed military regulations to govern the appearance of troops at this time we must draw general conclusions about their arms and equipment.

The man-at-arms of lower rank was usually armed with a lance, sword, mace or war hammer. He would have the traditional heater-shaped shield. His body would be protected by a hauberk or 'jack' extending to the mid-thigh or even knees, and having sleeves which hung to the elbow. This garment would typically be strengthened by any of the numerous forms of jazerant-work or banded mail. Additional protection might be given at the shoulders, elbows and knees by roundels, caps or plates, while two mamelières might protect the chest in place of a breast plate. The limbs might be

covered by greaves and vambraces of leather strengthened with splints of iron and thick leather gauntlets; shoes protected the feet. On the head was a bascinet, with perhaps a camail or a skull cap of banded mail. Beneath the hauberk or jack was a gambeson or leather tunic.

The billman or pikeman was usually well protected, the better-off men wearing mail hauberks, quilted gambesons or brigandines with metal-scale reinforcement. Their helmets varied considerably from skull caps composed of two pieces of metal riveted together with reinforcing strips of metal, to wide-brimmed 'hats' of iron, and even the fashionable sallet with its projecting tail to protect the wearer's neck. Their head protection was rarely extended to cover the face. The more fortunate foot soldiers would have plate roundels at the shoulders or elbows, or even a single metal breast plate strapped over the shoulders and around the waist, the straps perhaps crossing at the back like a pair of braces. After any successful engagement foot soldiers would collect pieces of armour and weapons off the enemy corpses, and as a general rule we might speculate that the knightly defence of one period became the common soldiers' protection in the next.

Few foot soldiers carried large shields, tending to rely on the small round buckler which could be hung on the sword hilt or belt. Most infantry carried a dual-purpose cut-and-thrust sword at their hip, and troops not trained as archers carried a glaive, pike or bill; these descendants of agricultural implements were now improved and sophisticated, and were used to great effect by the infantry of the early 15th century. In addition to these weapons some men had axes and mallets, particularly archers, who used them to kill the French knights at Agincourt when the fighting came to close combat.

The Longbow

The longbow was such a decisive weapon at Agincourt that it deserves a special mention.

The cradle of the longbow was South Wales,

and it was some time before the importance of this weapon was really appreciated by the English. Richard I and King John preferred to employ mercenaries with crossbows, and use Welsh men-at-arms but not Welsh archers. But when Edward I turned his attention towards Scotland after his conquest of Wales the longbow became a significant weapon in his army, until finally at Falkirk, 1298, a mixed force of English and Welsh archers soundly defeated the Scottish pikemen, and the decisive potential of missile weapons used en masse was fully appreciated. The battle of Falkirk marked the beginning of the English practice of closely combining archers and men-at-arms that was to shape the course of European

Detail of the head of the 11th Earl of Oxford's effigy, showing the richly decorated orle round the pointed bascinet. In the normal convention, his head is pillowed on his crested 'great helm'.

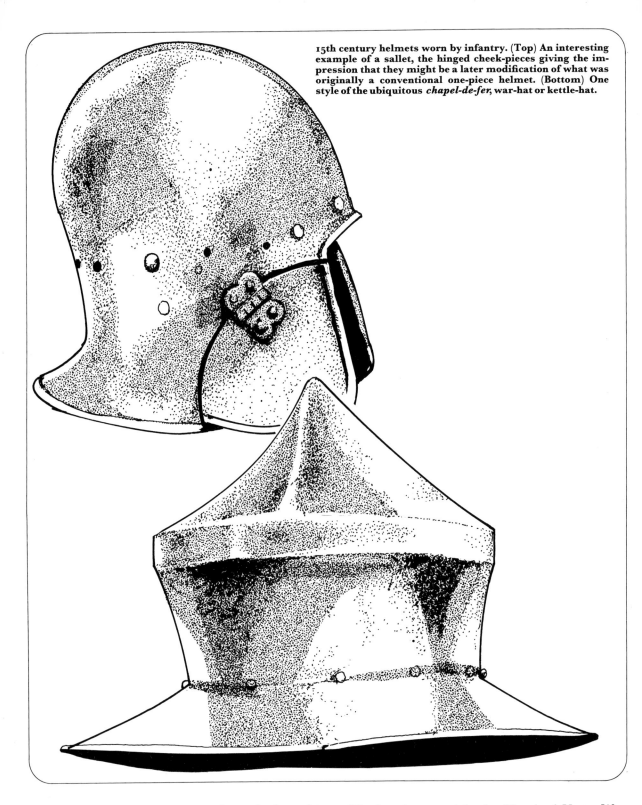

history for the next 150 years, and was the first of a series of victories that was to include Duplin Moor, Halidon Hill, Morlaix, Crécy, Poitiers, Najera and finally Agincourt.

The longbow used in the Hundred Years War was at its best when made from local or imported Spanish yew; but other woods, though always considered of secondary quality, were used, especially at times when it was feared that our supplies of local yew could be exhausted. The elm, ash and wych-hazel were regarded as good substitutes for yew. The bows were between $5\frac{1}{2}$ and $6\frac{1}{2}$ feet long, tapering towards the ends from the centre, with a slot or 'nock' cut at each end to take the linen string. It is possible but by no means certain that some military longbows had horn nocks. When the bow was not in use the string was removed and was carefully protected from the weather. Bows seem sometimes to have been carried unstrung in tubular canvas covers for the same reason. The bows of Agincourt were probably between 80lb and 120lb draw-weight, achieving ranges of approximately 300 yards, this varying with the weight of the arrowhead.

Arrows were about 36 inches long and were drawn back to the ear. The flights were usually made of duck or goose feathers, but sometimes parchment or even peacock feathers were used. Many types of wood were employed in the manufacture of the arrow shaft including brazil, hornbeam, birch, ash, oak, blackthorn and beech. Ash was favoured by the military archer because it was reasonably easy to obtain, and made heavy shafts which struck with greater weight and therefore gave deeper penetration.

As armour improved, so the archer resourcefully modified his arrows, so that by the end of the 13th century broad-headed arrows were being replaced by a four-sided, lozenge or chisel-pointed 'bodkin'. This varied in length from two to five inches. Mail provided little protection against it, and as tests have proved, it was capable of penetrating the plate armour of the 14th and early 15th centuries.

The secret of the archer's skill lay in his constant practice with the weapon. The training started in childhood and as the young archer increased his strength so it was matched with an increasingly powerful bow. The authorities passed ordinances to ensure that archery was practised continuously and to the exclusion of other sports and pastimes. Virtually every village in England had its butts where most Sundays and feastdays were passed in the pursuit of excellence with longbow, until eventually every shire in England could provide a given number of archers to serve in the king's wars.

Finally, it is interesting to note the gradual growth of English confidence in the combination of men-at-arms and archers. During the reign of Edward III the proportion was usually about two archers to each man-at-arms. At Agincourt this proportion had increased to five-to-one and, 20 years later, it rose to six, seven, or even ten bows to each lance.

Artillery

The guns employed by the French at Agincourt had little significance on the final outcome of the

(Top) One reconstruction of the Oriflamme, the sacred red banner of the Abbey of St Denis, carried by the French kings as vassals of the abbey for the fief of the Vexin since 1088. It was taken from the abbey in time of war and carried before the French army in battle. Many versions, differing widely, are shown in MS illustrations and stained glass windows. Some have three, some five, some eight tails. Some are plain red; some, as here, are described as having green trim and tassels; some are charged with gold flames or stars. At least two examples are known to have been lost in battle, so different versions are unsurprising. All, however, are *gonfanons*, and not *gonfalons* hung from a crossbar. At Agincourt the bearer of the Oriflamme, Guillaume Martel, was killed fighting in the front rank of the first French division. After Agincourt there seems to be only one isolated mention of the use of the Oriflamme, in 1465. (Bottom) Banner of the Duke of Orleans, a fierce-looking black heraldic 'hedgehog' on a white field.

Another view of the effigy of Lord Bardolf. Note the gauntlets with gadlings and engraved fingernails. Fan-shaped plates protect the armpits; these are more normally round or oval, sometimes decorated with St George's cross.

conflict. But their appearance marked the beginning of the end of the armoured horseman, and they would eventually lead to a complete change in the pattern of war.

Perhaps the earliest known use of guns in European warfare is recorded by an order in the Council of Florence as early as 1326; and, at virtually the same time, an illustration in a manuscript belonging to Edward III shows a strange bottle-shaped gun about to fire an arrow. Presumably the bulbous section at the rear of the barrel was made thicker because this was where the powder would explode. During the next half-century artillery was rapidly improved, so that by 1377 the great chronicler Froissart mentions a gun firing a ball of 200lb at the siege of Ardres.

It is doubtful if these large guns were ever cast in single units, and it seems more likely that they were manufactured by beating iron strips together lengthways around a cylindrical former; heated iron hoops were slid along the outside of the barrel and, in cooling, would shrink to grip and further strengthen the barrel. A separate iron chamber to accommodate the powder was removable (by various methods) from the breech end. Artilleries of the period began to experiment with different sized cannons. Smaller guns were often breech-loaders, but the larger guns of the period are shown lying on the ground with a large wooden frame behind them and seem to have been too big to have a removable breech.

Handguns, too, made their appearance during this period. In 1364 the Italian town of Perugia bought 500 small guns, each of which could be fired in the hands of an individual soldier. These were probably short-barrelled weapons, cast in one piece and held by means of a wooden shaft which fitted into a socket at the rear of the barrel. The operator would hold the shaft with one hand and light the touch hole with the other, perhaps using a wall or tree to rest the barrel on.

It has been suggested that the Genoese cross-bowmen at Crécy were frightened by English guns, though we are still not at all certain that there were any guns at Crécy. We do know, however, that Edward III used artillery the following year when he layed siege to Calais. By the time Henry V started his invasion of France the use of artillery by medieval armies was an established practice, though still regarded by some as a violation of the code of chivalry. We know that Henry did not join this school of thought, because listed in his retinue for France were 75 gunners led by four master gunners, all of them Dutchmen; and later we hear of Henry taking a personal interest in the preparations for the thrice-daily bombardments of Harfleur. By 1424 the English artillery was so effective that it battered down the walls of Le Mans in a matter of days.

Guns used by both sides were becoming more efficient but still lacked the important property of mobility. Many large guns were fired on the ground from behind a frame with a large hinged flap, which protected the gunners and could be raised to expose the muzzle when the gun came into action. Some smaller weapons were mounted and fired on carts, the more sophisticated of these being multi-barrelled. But by the early 15th century by far the commonest form of artillery was the breech loader, which was fired on the ground. This had a removable breech, cylindrical in shape with a large handle, and at the rear a touch hole. This chamber held the powder and was placed in the barrel behind the ball and held firmly by wedges beaten into position behind it.

Analysis of the Battle

After examining the relative sizes and physical condition of the two armies it is difficult to understand how the English won and the French lost, and why the outcome was so totally one-sided. An account of the course of the battle shows how great a part was played by the massive firepower of the English archers, and underlines the fact that they, unrestricted by armour, could fight effectively at close quarters with their side-arms when the French men-at-arms penetrated the English lines. Neither must we underestimate the courage of the English men-at-arms upon whom the full weight of the French first attack was directed. But these factors alone did not bring about the English victory.

The English had two major advantages. Firstly, Henry was in personal command, and there was something about his manner and confidence that made him loved and respected by his men. The

(Top) Standard of the House of Bourbon: white on blue cross of St Denis in the hoist; the fly divided white over green, barred with the motto 'Esperance' in black on gold strips bordered black, and charged with red flames, green and white thistles on the white and green areas respectively, and a gold flying stag. (Bottom) The standard of the Constable of France: gold lillies on a white field. This would have been taken into battle and flown close to D'Albret's position.

authority he exercised over his army during its period in France was exceptional for armies of this time. However, we must acknowledge that his march from Harfleur to Calais was a gamble to say the least, and the French skilfully out-manoeuvred him at every point from Harfleur to Agincourt. So it is clear that Henry was better at retrieving situations than creating them. The battle at Agincourt was just such a situation.

The second advantage the English had was the proportion of archers to men-at-arms. It was the best possible ratio for the strategy adopted by the English army. The French should have exploited this; the longbow is essentially a weapon of

Contemporary drawings of gunners: (top) is a well-armoured soldier, with plate defences on the legs as well as the upper body. Note that the 'tiller' or stock of the hand-gun is rested on top of the shoulder—to fire this kind of weapon braced against the shoulder in the modern manner would have been to invite disaster. Note the use of a fuse. (Bottom) is an artilleryman wearing a helmet, and what appears to be a breastplate over a brigandine over chain mail. He holds the removable chamber of a cannon, but the artist seems to have omitted the cavity for it in the barrel.

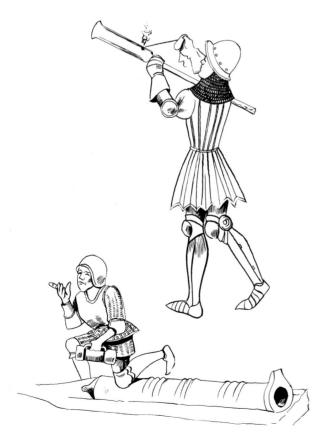

defence, and the French could have withdrawn and allowed the English to exhaust themselves in useless pursuit, or surrounded them in Maison-celles and allowed them to starve to death.

The French neutralised their great numerical advantage by confining their attack to the narrow bottleneck between the woods of Agincourt and Tramecourt, thus packing themselves too closely and making themselves more vulnerable to the dense showers of English arrows, and creating such tight formations that they could not lift their arms to use their weapons. Perhaps this form of attack had been based on their fairly recent victory over the Flemish infantry at Roosebeck in 1382. At this battle the French had combined a frontal attack by dismounted men-at-arms with a simultaneous attack on both flanks by mounted knights. The tremendous pressure from three sides cramped the Flemish so much that their defence collapsed and many troops were crushed or suffocated to death. If the French hoped for a similar outcome at Agincourt they had foolishly ignored the protection given to both English flanks by the two woods. In addition to selecting a bad position to fight their battle, the French also sent their heavily armoured mounted and dismounted men-at-arms across rain-soaked ground which they quickly trans-formed into a morass, so that by the time they arrived at the English lines they had exhausted themselves *en route*.

Finally, the political situation in France strongly influenced the outcome of the battle. Besides dividing the French command structure and creating family jealousies and rival allegiances, the continuous animosity between the Armagnacs and Burgundians created an instability within France that prevented the nation meeting the English with a unified front.

The Plates

A1: Crossbowman
This illustration shows a well-armed crossbow-man. He carries his pavise by means of two straps crossing his chest. On his head he wears an iron *chapel-de-fer* helmet and a mail coif. The shoulders and armpits are given additional protection by

using steel plates and roundels. His body is protected by a quilted gambeson and a plackart, a form of half-breast plate which protected the vulnerable abdominal area without excessively restricting movement. The windlass and short quiver are attached to his belt; note the bolts, or quarrels, are carried flight downwards.

A2: English archer

This illustration shows a well-equipped English archer. Fortunate archers had some form of armour, perhaps a hauberk, quilted gambeson or brigandine jacket. A few would wear a helmet, such as a *chapel-de-fer*, although a bascinet or sallet, with its lack of brim and greater neck protection, was a more suitable headdress for archers. Many archers had no head protection at all, while others wore conical hats of boiled leather or tarpaulin over a wickerwork frame, strengthened by strips of iron.

It should perhaps be mentioned that at least one account suggests that some archers may have fought at Agincourt virtually naked below the waist. The dysentery which was rife among the army on the march from Harfleur had led some to remove their hose altogether, to ease the miserable business of constantly falling out by the roadside to surrender to the demands of that most demoralising disease. It seems probable that the worst-afflicted would still have presented a squalid and pitiable spectacle at Agincourt—although we may also speculate that the psychological disadvantages of going into battle without one's trousers were as well appreciated in the 15th century as the 20th!

Some form of hand-to-hand weapon seems normally to have been carried as well as the bow. Note also the red cross of St George simply sewn to the brigandine—it was probably displayed in some form or other by most of the English soldiers.

A3: Infantryman

This illustration shows a well-equipped infantryman of the period. He is typical of many of the regular garrison troops fighting in the French army at the battle. His primary weapon is a glaive, a long spear-like weapon with a cutting edge. On his head he wears a *chapel-de-fer* and beneath this a mail coif. His chest and upper arms are protected by a mail shirt worn beneath a

Contemporary drawings of guns. (Top) is a crude but informative view of a gunner wearing an apparently quilted jacket with mail and a helmet, holding the firing wire or fuse of a small gun strapped with iron bands to its wooden base. (Bottom) is a much more elaborate gun of the later 15th century, with an elevating mechanism. The gunner wears a plackart or half-breastplate.

leather jerkin. He has some plate armour protection over the vulnerable knees and plate roundels over the shoulder joints. On his belt is strapped a sword and buckler.

B1: Thomas, Lord Camoys, KG

The commander of the English left wing at Agincourt; we take this illustration from his brass at Trotton, Sussex, dated 1419. No surcoat is worn, and we can see that complete plate has now superseded mail. The bascinet, not so acutely pointed at the apex as previously, has an elegant trefoil decoration across the forehead. This is repeated on the gorget, the lowest tace of the skirt

or fauld, and on the gauntlets. Large roundels protect the armpits, and fluted fin-like plates cover the vulnerable elbow joints. The horizontal sword belt so typical of the late 14th century has now been succeeded by a diagonal belt, here ornamented with quatrefoils, as is the scabbard of the sword. A dagger is attached to a short cord passing through a loop fastened in the lowest of the six taces. Arms: Or, on a chief Gules three roundels Argent.

B2: King Henry V
Henry succeeded his father Henry IV at the age of 25, with a reputation as a frivolous roisterer. By the time he died at the age of 34 he was a hero to his people and admired throughout Europe. His love of soldiering does not seem to have distracted him seriously from the other aspects of administering the kingdom, which is more than can be said of some other medieval monarchs. There is no doubt that he was cruel and ruthless—in a cruel age—in his treatment both of Lollard religious dissenters, and of prisoners of war. It was his firm intention to make himself master of all France, and then to lead an Anglo-French army on a new crusade against the Turks. He studied reports of harbours in Syria and Egypt, and a history of the First Crusade was at his bedside when he died. Arms: Quarterly, France Modern and England.

Note the insignia of the Order of the Garter worn at the left calf by all the figures on this page; and the collars of 'S' shapes, indicating office under the House of Lancaster.

B3: William Phelipp, Lord Bardolf, KG
This illustration of the Lieutenant of Calais is based on the beautiful alabaster effigy in St Mary's Church at Dennington in Suffolk. Lord Bardolf wears complete plate with carefully articulated joints and smooth, glancing surfaces. The camail has been replaced by a deep gorget of plate. Narrow overlapping plates—épaulières—cover the shoulders, and pointed, fan-shaped plates

Brass of Sir John Wylcotes, 1410, at Great Tew, Oxfordshire. Mail shows beneath the gorget and taces; the baviére and bascinet are shown as overlapping the gorget, but one should not take all details of such brasses too literally. The appearance of the armpit defences suggests that they may originally have borne painted decoration of some type.

guard the elbow joints. The gauntlets, deeper than those of the late 14th century, still have the beautiful jewelled gadlings. The sword belt crosses the fauld of taces at a diagonal, but a broad, jewelled, horizontal dagger belt is still worn. Note on B2 and B3 the use of the orle, the padded ring of fabric around the bascinet. Its appearance suggests that it originated in a simple pad to ease the fitting of the great helm over the bascinet in the days when both were normally worn together. The richly embroidered and jewelled decoration may suggest that its use was by this time largely decorative.

C1: English man-at-arms

The men-at-arms, using the term in the sense of the poorer armoured cavalry of the army, varied a great deal in their appearance, and we may assume that good armour but of old-fashioned design was fairly common among them. This man, dismounted for foot combat at Agincourt, wears a snout-faced bascinet and a heavy camail. Beneath the white surcoat with the cross of St George, ordered for use by the whole army, he wears a quilted gambeson. His feet are unarmoured, and a good deal of mail is still evident in his armour. His primary weapon is a halberd, with a hook for dismounting riders and a broad, pointed blade for chopping and stabbing when the victim was down. He also carries a sword and dagger.

C2: Mountjoy, King of Arms

This herald wears a tabard emblazoned with the arms of his sovereign, Charles VI of France— France Modern. He wears contemporary civilian clothes with long riding boots, and carries a leather satchel for writing materials. The name 'Mountjoy' stems from the old national war-cry of France: 'Montjoie, St Denis!' In Shakespeare's *Henry V* he gives Mountjoy the duty of telling Henry that the day is his, and asking permission to draw up the roll of the dead. The herald was a privileged non-combatant, much used as an intermediary.

C3: Garter King of Arms

This illustration shows William Bruges, first 'Garter King of Arms', appointed in January 1420; it is based on a manuscript illustration in the

An MS illustration apparently dating from the first quarter of the 15th century shows an interesting mixture of helmet styles in use simultaneously; although this is specifically a battle picture, rather than a tourney, we see a 'great helm' alongside old-fashioned open-face bascinets, and a bascinet with added gorget of plate.

Bodleian Library. Bruges had previously been Guienne King of Arms, and had served (with Lancaster King at Arms and Ireland King at Arms) at Agincourt. So great was the importance of the victory felt to be that Henry created a new title for a herald, 'Agincourt', and granted him lands for life. The official dress of the herald, the tabard, has remained virtually unchanged down the centuries.

D1: Jean le Meingre, dit 'Boucicaut', Marshal of France

This illustration is based on a contemporary painting in a Book of Hours, *Les Heures de Maréchal de Boucicaut*, of *c.*1410–15. He wears a beautiful long-sleeved jupon emblazoned with the arms he wore at his wedding; his normal arms were Argent, a two-headed eagle displayed Gules, with beaks and legs Azure. Note the method of displaying these arms halved on the torso and complete, but smaller, on the sleeve. His neck is protected by a small 'standard'—collar—of mail with a decorated edge. The sabatons on the feet are long, pointed and flexible, and have long spurs secured to them by a decorated, buckled strap. It is interesting to note the fashion for short hair, cut in a close fringe around the head, possibly for comfort when wearing armour.

D2: Charles d'Albret, Constable of France

Over his armour the constable wears a loose-fitting, long-sleeved surcoat emblazoned with his arms—France Modern, quarterly with Gules, which symbolises the fact that he was second cousin to the king. The bascinet is more globular in outline than in the late 14th century, but is still pointed at the apex. The lower portion which had now been added to protect the chin was known as a bavière. The earlier form of hinged, snout-faced visor was now being replaced by a blunter and more rounded form with a prominent swelling over nose and mouth. The sword is a long hand-and-a-half type, a double-edged weapon used both for cutting and thrusting.

D3: Charles, Duke of Orleans

Charles is protected by a complete harness of plate. The deep gorget has replaced the mail camail of the earlier period, and the developing skill of the armourer is displayed by the way in which the metal curves of the convex bavière and the concave gorget are articulated, allowing the head to move within the collar while still giving complete protection. The jupon, closer in cut to the tabard of a later period, is emblazoned with

Brass of Sir John Leventhorpe, 1433, at Sawbridgeworth Church, Hertfordshire. A complete suit of plate, with the lowest tace suspended from straps.

the arms France Modern and a label Argent. He wears no visible sword belt, but one is clearly worn beneath the jupon, which is slit to give free access to the weapons.

E1: Richard de Vere, Earl of Oxford

This illustration is based on the alabaster tomb effigy of the 11th Earl of Oxford in St Stephen's Chapel at Bures in Suffolk. The armour is that of *c.*1400–10, a transitional style in which the plate gorget is worn over a camail. The tight jupon is slightly shorter than usually seen, and through it the form of the taces can be made out. It is emblazoned with the arms: Quarterly Gules and Or, in the first quarter a mullet Argent. The pointed bascinet, fitted with a jewelled orle, is decorated above the brow in brass, gilt or lateen. Concave plates, to trap enemy points, protect the armpits, and roundels are worn at the elbows.

E2: Sir Thomas Erpingham, KG

Born in 1357, Sir Thomas was an elderly man by the time he distinguished himself as commander of the bowmen at Agincourt; he is recorded as having white hair. The illustration is based on the statue of Sir Thomas above the Erpingham Gate at Norwich Cathedral. He is shown bare-headed, with a long beard, and wearing a fairly long heraldic jupon which fits loosely and has very short, scalloped 'cap' sleeves. His armour is slightly old-fashioned, in the late 14th century style, with mail visible at the neck and below the jupon. He holds a baton, indicating his position of command. The plain white 'heater' shield in the centre of his blazon is surrounded by eight white birds.

E3: Sir Edmund de Thorpe

A well-known soldier, Sir Edmund died in 1418, apparently at the siege of Louviers. Here he is armed with a war-hammer for dismounted combat. The main points of the illustration are taken from the alabaster effigy in Ashwellthorpe Church, Norfolk. His armour is a classic example of the transitional period: a cuirass covered by a

Much larger roundels at the armpits, and more elaborate fluted elbow defences, are seen in the brass of Sir Robert Suckling (?), *c.*1415, at Barsham, Suffolk. Note the dagger.

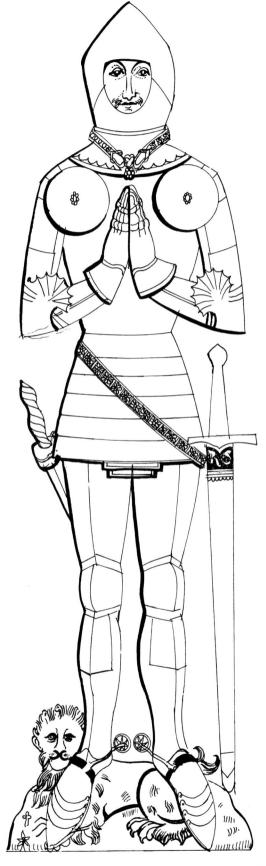

tight jupon, a hauberk, a camail worn beneath a gorget of plate, a bascinet with baviére, articulated shoulder-pieces, brassarts, elbow-cops, vambraces, taces, knee-cops, jambs and solerets. On the effigy the hands are in the position of prayer, with deeply-cuffed gauntlets and jewelled gadlings. The narrow diagonal sword belt supports a hand-and-a-half sword, and is worn over a deeper dagger belt of traditional design. The head of the effigy rests on a tilting helm, crested with a panache of peacock feathers. The arms are those of Thorpe (Azure, three crescents Argent) quartered with those of his mother, the daughter and heiress of Robert Baynard (Sable, a fess between two chevrons Or).

F: Sir John Codrington, Standard Bearer to Henry V

Sir John's armour is of the transitional type, the older features being the snout-faced bascinet and the fringe of mail visible beneath the taces. It is decorated with brass borders and ornamentation, and worn with a short, tight heraldic jupon. This, and the horse bardings, display Sir John's arms: Argent, a fess between three lions passant guardant Gules. The horse is protected by a chamfron covering the face and brow, and a crinet covering the neck with a series of articulated plates.

G1: Hand gunner

The hand guns of the early 15th century were simply small, crude cannons fixed by metal straps or by socketing to a wooden shaft. The weapon was usually fired with the shaft braced into the ground at a low angle, hooked to a wall or other convenient support, or rested on top of the shoulder—the recoil was too great for bracing against the shoulder to be practically possible.

G2: Edward, Duke of Bar

A transitional armour blending features of the earlier, camail-and-jupon period with the later, complete-plate-without-surcoat period. The camail, the other areas of mail and the relatively simple design of the elbow and knee plates may all be considered early features. In fact a surcoat is worn, and is seen in the background; for a detailed illustration of the arms of the Dukes of Bar (Azure, semy of cross-crosslet fitchy, two barbels nauriant addorsed Or) see Men-at-Arms 111, *The Armies of*

Crécy and Poitiers, Plate D3. Note the fauld of five taces, and the interesting 'split' construction of the breast plate.

G3: Artilleryman

The protective armour worn by this gunner may be as much to guard against the hazards of flashbacks, weak barrels, and all the other accidents associated with the dawn of gunnery, as against the weapons of the enemy. He carries a removable gun chamber. This was filled with powder and placed in a cut-out in the breech of the barrel, with a ball placed in the opening of the barrel just in front. Wedges were hammered in behind the chamber to make a tight fit, and the gun would then be fired by thrusting a red-hot wire on a wooden pole into the touch-hole. The crude, massively constructed guns of the day were fixed with metal straps or lashings to heavy wooden bases, and were only mobile when loaded onto wagons; they were thus of little use against any target other than a static fortification.

H1: Mounted archer

The first experiment in the use of light cavalry in English armies was made in 1296 when Edward I included 260 Irish hobilars in his army in Scotland. By 1333, Edward III was beginning to find that he required mounted archers to provide mobile firepower on the battlefield. These were the first 'dragoons', in the sense that they rode into battle, dismounted, and formed up to use their bows on foot. They proved far more effective than hobilars, and completely replaced them in English armies; they were paid higher wages than foot archers. The figure illustrated is armed with the usual long self-wood bow, a quiver of arrows and a sword and buckler—the small concave shield with a crossbar grip. He wears a padded jack, long riding boots, protective gauntlets, and an iron-framed 'kettle hat' with hardened leather inserts.

Two views of the superb effigy of Richard Beauchamp, Earl of Warwick, who died in 1439. The development of the armour in the generation after Agincourt may be seen in the appearance of the enlarged shoulder-pieces with high flanges to protect the neck. The asymmetrical features stem from the abandonment of the shield and the reinforcement and enlargement of the plates on the left arm and left side of the torso, the side presented to the enemy in tourneys. Note the care with which the 'pudding basin' haircut has been rendered.

H2, H3: Crossbowmen

To protect the crossbowman during the rather slow and awkward business of reloading, he was usually equipped with a shield known as a pavise which he carried into battle and set up in front of him with a prop of some kind, either a simple stake or a pivoted bar permanently fixed to the pavise. On the inside face are sometimes found iron staples for carrying straps, and leather grips. Various types of painted decoration are often seen, including quite elaborate heraldic designs.

As crossbows became more powerful, so the means of spanning them improved. The windlass —see Plate A1—was efficient but slow, and its complicated arrangement of miniature 'blocks and tackles' was obviously vulnerable to campaign conditions. The 'bending lever' was obviously superior; it was simple, robust, and allowed the bowman to keep under cover. There were two main types, one 'pushing' the string on to the release nut and the other 'pulling' it; H2 illustrates a 'puller'.

Notes sur les planches en couleur

A1 Arbalétrier bien protégé de son armure, portant son pavise sur le dos et son ressort à la ceinture. **A2** Archer bien équipé; la plupart des archers à Agincourt portaient une armure succinte, faite d'une veste matelassée et peut être également un simple casque. La plupart des soldats anglais portaient la croix rouge fixée sur leurs habits. **A3** Fantassin français bien équipé, armé d'un glaive.

B1 Le commandant de l'aile gauche anglaise portant une armure à plates typique du début du 15ème siècle; d'après son effigie mortuaire datant de 1419. **B2** On pense que le casque se trouvant aux pieds du roi était porté par dessus le bascinet pendant la bataille. Notez l'insigne de l'ordre de la Jarretière porté à la jambe gauche par chacun des personnages sur cette illustration. **B3** Le lieutenant de Calais; d'après son effigie mortuaire. Notez, sur les bascinets montrés à B2 et B3, les orles rembourrés et décorés de très belle façon. Ceux-ci avaient probablement commencé en tant que simples rembourrages pour maintenir le casque en place, quand il était porté par dessus le bascinet.

C1 Armure à l'ancienne mode, typique des chevaliers de moindre rang d'Agincourt. La croix rouge est portée sur un jupon blanc, d'après l'ordre donné à l'armée toute entière. Pour le combat à pied, ce soldat porte une hallebarde. **C2** Le héraut porte un tabard brodé aux armes du roi Charles VI, et porte ses ustensiles d'écriture dans une sacoche; il devait en effet dresser la liste des morts. **C3** De même façon, le héraut anglais porte un tabard à armoires.

D1 Le jupon, brodé des armoires doubles portées par Boucicaut à son marriage, est inspiré d'une peinture de son Livre d'Heures personnel. **D2** La forme sphérique du bascinet est typique du début du 15ème siècle. Le gorget et la bavière—protections en plates du cou et du menton—ont maintenant remplacées la cotte de maille portée au 14ème siècle. **D3** Le gorget et le bascinet sont ajustés ensemble avec soin de façon à de que la tête puisse tourner sans obstacle à l'intérieur du gorget rigide.

E1 Une armure de transition, montrant des caractéristiques de la fin du 14ème —début du 15ème siècle, d'après l'effigie mortuaire du Comte. **E2** Le commandant âgé des archers anglais à Agincourt tient un bâton, insigne de commandement, et porte un jupon brodé de ses armoiries personnelles. **E3** Un chevalier éminent, qui mourut en 1418 au siège de Louviers; il porte un maillotin pour le combat à pied.

F Sir John porte l'armure de transition à bascinet à museau à l'ancienne mode et son jupon et caparaçon exhibent ses armouries personnelles. Il était le porte-drapeau du roi Henry à Agincourt.

G1 Le canon était tiré avec le fût reposant sur le sol ou bien à l'épaule. **G2** Notez l'assemblage en deux morceaux de la plate de poitrine. Le jupon porté par dessus cette armure est illustré dans Men-at-Arms 111, *The Armies of Crécy and Poitiers*, illustration D3. **G3** Les vêtements de protection et les armures étaient portés par les canoniers pour les protéger tout autant des accidents, inévitable à l'aube de cette artillerie primitive, que de l'ennemi.

H1 Les archers à cheval chevauchaient à la bataille, mais descendaient de cheval pour le combat. Ce soldat porte le cabasset, très commun, fait de cuir bouli à renforts de fer; une brigandine matelassée et des cuissardes. **H2, H3** Le pavise était souvent peint de motifs héraldiques. Le levier remplace le ressort qui était plus compliqué, pour bander l'arbalète; ce système était plus simple, plus sûr, et permettait à l'arbalète d'être rebandée pendant que l'archer restait à couvert.

Farbtafeln

A1 Ein gut gepanzerter Armbrustschütze, der seine pavise auf seinem Rücken und seine Winde an seinem Gürtel trägt. **A2** Ein gut ausgerüsteter Schütze; die meisten Bogenschützen bei Agincourt würden, ausser einer wattierten Jacke und vielleicht einem einfachen Helm, wenig Rüstung getragen haben. Das rote Kreuz wurde von den meisten englischen Soldaten an der Kleidung getragen. **A3** Ein gut ausgerüsteter französischer Infanterist, mit einer glaive bewaffnet.

B1 Der Kommandeur des englischen linken Flügels, in einem typischen Panzeranzug des frühen 15. Jahrhunderts; kopiert von seinem Grabbildnis, 1419. **B2** Man glaubt, dass der Helm, gezeigt bei den Füssen des Königs, während der Schlacht über dem bascinet getragen worden war. Bemerke das Abzeichen des Hosenbandordens, das von allen drei Figuren auf dieser Abbildung um das linke Bein getragen wird. **B3** Der Leutnant von Calais; kopiert von seinem Grabbildnis. Bemerke, auf den bascinets von B2 und B3, die wattierten und wunderschön verzierten orles—die wahrscheinlich ihren Ursprung darin hatten, um als einfache Wattierung den Helm in Position zu halten, wenn er gewöhnlich über dem bascinet getragen wurde.

C1 Altmodische Rüstung, typisch für die Ritter von niedrigerem Rang bei Agincourt. Das rote Kreuz wird auf einem weissen japon in der Art getragen, wie es für die ganze Armee befohlen war. Für den vom Pferd abgesessenen Kampf, trägt er eine Hellebarde. **C2** Der Herold trägt einen tabard, bestickt mit dem Wappen König Karls VI, und trägt eine Mappe mit Schreibzeug; zu seinen Pflichten gehörte das Aufzeichnen der Totenliste. **C3** Ahnlich, der englische Herold ist mit einem heraldischen tabard bekleidet.

D1 Der jupon, bestickt mit einem doppelten Satz der heraldischen Wappen, getragen von Boucicaut bei seiner Hochzeit, ist einem Gemälde in seinem persönlichen Stundenbuch entnommen. **D2** Die globusähnliche Form des bascinet ist typisch für das frühe 15. Jahrhundert. Das gorget und bavière—gepanzerter Schutz für Hals und Kinn—hatten nunmehr die Kettenpanzer-rüstung, die im 14. Jahrhundert getragen wurde, ersetzt. **D3** Bascinet und gorget sind mit grossem Geschick zusammengefügt, so dass der Kopf sich innerhalb des steifen gorgets frei drehen kann.

E1 Eine Panzerrüstung für den Übergang, Eigenheiten des späten 14./frühen 15. Jahrhunderts zeigend, dem Grabbildnis des Grafens entnommen. **E2** Der alternde Kommandeur der englischen Schützen bei Agincourt hält einen Stab, seine Befehlskraft anzeigend, und trägt einen mit seinem persönlichen Wappen bestickten jupon. **E3** Ein berühmter Ritter, der im Jahre 1418 bei der Belagerung von Louviers starb; er trägt einen Kriegshammer für den vom Pferd abgesessenen Kampf.

F Sir John trägt Übergangsrüstung mit einem altmodischen 'rüssel-besetztem bascinet', und sein jupon und sein Pferdeparadegeschirr zeigen sein persönliches Wappen. Er war der Standartenträger für König Henry bei Agincourt.

G1 Das Geschütz wurde mit dem Schafft auf dem Boden oder oben auf der Schulter ruhend abgefeuert. **G2** Bemerke die zweiteilige Konstruktion der Brustplatte, Der jupon, getragen über diese Rüstung, ist abgebildet in Men-at-Arms 111, *The Armies of Crécy and Poitiers*, Tafel D3. **G3** Die schützende Kleidung und Rüstung ist genauso sehr zum Schutz des Schützen gegen Unfälle, unvermeidlich in den Anfängen der primitiven Artillerie, als auch vor dem Feind, getragen.

H1 Die berittenen Schützen ritten in die Schlacht, sassen jedoch zum Kampf ab. Dieser Soldat trägt den gewöhnlichen 'Kesselhut', aus gehärtetem Leder mit eiserner Verstärkung; eine wattierte brigandine; und lange Reitstiefel. **H2, H3** Die pavise war oft reichlich bemalt mit heraldischen Motiven. Der Hebel ersetzte die kompliziertere Winde als das Ladegerät für die Armbrust; er war einfacher, führte zu wenigeren Unfällen und erlaubte, dass der Bogen gespannt werden konnte, während der Schütze in Deckung blieb.